BIRDS

Spotted Owls

James E. Gerholdt
ABDO & Daughters

Published by Abdo & Daughters, 4940 Viking Drive, Suite 622, Edina, Minnesota 55435.

Copyright © 1997 by Abdo Consulting Group, Inc., Pentagon Tower, P.O. Box 36036, Minneapolis, Minnesota 55435 USA. International copyrights reserved in all countries. No part of this book may be reproduced in any form without written permission from the publisher.

Printed in the United States.

Cover and Interior Photo credits: Peter Arnold, Inc.

Edited by Julie Berg

Library of Congress Cataloging-in-Publication Data

Gerholdt, James E., 1943—
        Spotted owls/James E. Gerholdt.
                p.   cm. -- (birds)
        Includes index.
        Summary: Describes the physical characteristics, habitat, and habits of the owl which needs to live in a forest that has not been logged and in which the trees are old.
        ISBN 1-56239-589-0
        1. Spotted owls--Juvenile literature. [1. Spotted owls. 2. Owls.] I. Title. II. Series: Gerholdt, James E., 1943—Birds.
        Ql696.S83G47   1996
        598.9'7--dc20   95-48187
                                                               CIP
                                                               AC

Second printing 2002

Contents

SPOTTED OWLS

Spotted owls belong to one of the 28 **orders** of **birds**. There are two **families** of owls: the typical owls and the barn owls. The spotted owl is a typical owl, and is a **nocturnal** bird of prey. Birds are **vertebrates**. This means they have backbones, just like humans. Birds are also **warm-blooded**.

Spotted owls are an **endangered species**, which means they are in danger of extinction. To protect the spotted owls, **logging** is not allowed in their **habitat.**

Opposite page: A northern spotted owl on a branch.

SIZES

Spotted owls are medium-sized **birds**. The females are a little larger than the males, and their average weight is 1 pound, 7 ounces (640 g). The males' average weight is 1 pound, 5 ounces (580 g).

From the tip of the beak to the tip of the tail, spotted owls can measure 16 1/2 to 19 inches (41 to 48 cm). The **wingspan** is about 45 inches (1.14 m).

Opposite page: A spotted owl in flight.

SHAPES

The spotted owl, like all of the owls, is a heavy-bodied **bird**, with long powerful wings. The head is round, with large eyes that face forward and are surrounded by a **facial disc**.

The neck looks short, but is actually long under the **feathers**. This long neck allows the owl to turn its head 180 degrees and look behind itself.

The feathers are soft and fluffy, and that is why the owl is able to fly so quietly. The tail is long and the legs are also covered with feathers.

There are four toes on each foot. The outer toe can face forward or backward. Powerful **talons** on the feet are used for catching **prey**, or for defense.

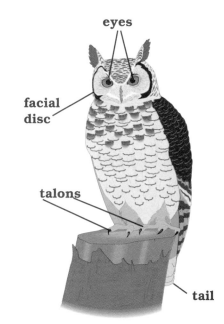

eyes

facial disc

talons

tail

8

A spotted owl fledgling holding prey in its claws.

COLORS

Male and female spotted owls have dark-brown **feathers** and eyes. All other North American owls, except the barred owl and the barn owl, have yellow eyes.

Like its name suggests, the spotted owl has white spots on its chest. The belly and tail, however, are striped. The beak and the feet are light colored.

Opposite page: A northern spotted owl has white spots on its chest.

WHERE THEY LIVE

Spotted owls are found in the Pacific Coast region of western North America, from southwestern British Columbia in Canada to central Mexico. They are also found in Utah, Arizona, New Mexico, and extreme west Texas.

Spotted owls live in wooded canyons and **coniferous, old-growth forests**. Areas of forest have been closed in order to protect these **birds**.

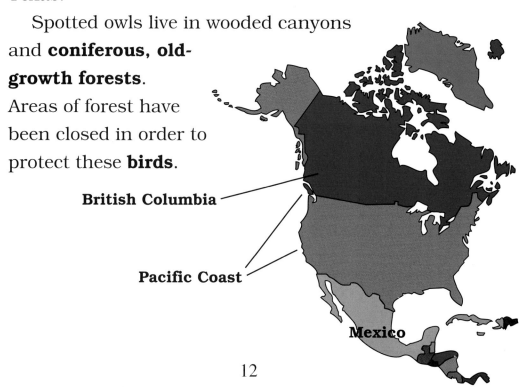

British Columbia

Pacific Coast

Mexico

A spotted owl living in the Pacific Northwest.

SENSES

Spotted owls have the same five senses as humans. Their senses of taste and smell are not very good. But these senses are not very important to them.

Spotted owls, like all owls, need their sight and hearing to find food. Their eyes are very large, and have a third eyelid to protect them from the bright daylight.

The spotted owl's ears are holes in the side of the head, surrounded by soft **feathers**. These feathers can be spread to make a "funnel," which helps sound reach the ear. The **facial discs** also help the owl to hear by collecting and sharpening sounds.

Opposite page: Spotted owls have great eyesight and hearing.

DEFENSE

The brown and white colors of the spotted owls help them to blend in with their surroundings. This is called **camouflage**, and is an important way to protect themselves from their enemies.

The spotted owl's keen eyesight and hearing will also warn it that an enemy is near. If the enemy gets too close, the owl can fly to a safe place. If all else fails, the feet and powerful **talons** are used for defense against enemies.

Opposite page: Spotted owls have sharp claws, and their color helps them to blend in with their surroundings.

FOOD

The spotted owl hunts at dusk or after dark. It will eat just about anything small enough to kill. **Prey** is grabbed with the **talons** and eaten.

A few of the prey animals include wood rats, deer mice, red tree mice, bats, and small **birds**. Even pygmy owls and screech owls are sometimes a meal. Insects such as moths, crickets, and large beetles also may wind up in the spotted owls' stomachs.

Opposite page: An owl with prey in its talons.

BABIES

All spotted owls hatch from eggs that have white, rough shells. These eggs are medium-sized, and measure 1 1/2 by 2 inches (41 x 50 mm). Two eggs are often laid at one time. But sometimes three or four are laid.

The nest is a hole in a cliff or a tree, or sometimes the old nest of a raven or hawk. Bare floors of caves or the bare ground at the base of a large rock are also used for nests. There are usually only a few **feathers** around the eggs for protection.

Opposite page: Spotted owls,
mother (right) and young.

GLOSSARY

bird (BURD) - A feathered animal with a backbone whose front limbs are wings.

camouflage (CAM-a-flaj) - The ability to blend in with the surroundings.

coniferous (kuh-NIFF-er-us) - Trees with cones, such as a pine tree.

endangered (en-DAIN-jerd) - Almost extinct.

facial disc (FAY-shull disk) - The flattened area around the eyes of an owl.

family (FAM-i-lee) - A grouping of animals ranked below an order.

feather (FETH-ur) - The light, flat structures covering a bird's body.

habitat (HAB-uh-tat) - The place where an animal lives.

logging (LOG-ing) - The cutting down of trees.

nocturnal (nok-TURN-al) - Active at night.

old-growth forest - An old forest that has not been logged.

order (OAR-der) - A grouping of animals, ranked higher than a family.

prey (PRAY) - Animals caught and killed for food.

species (SPEE-sees) - A kind or type.

talons (TAL-ons) - The claws of a raptor.

vertebrate (VER-tuh-brit) - An animal with a backbone.

warm-blooded (warm-BLUD-ed) - Regulating body temperature at a constant level, from inside the body.

wingspan (WING-span) - The distance from the tip of one wing to the other.

INDEX